Listen, **bitch**

Previous joint publications

1962: Be Spoken To (artist book) (2017)
Members Only (poetry volume) (Recent Work Press, 2017)

Other publications by Melinda Smith

Goodbye, Cruel (Pitt Street Poetry, 2017)
Drag down to unlock or place an emergency call (Pitt Street Poetry, 2013)
First..., Then... (Ginninderra Press, 2012)
Mapless in Underland (Ginninderra Press, 2004)
Pushing thirty, wearing seventeen (Ginninderra Press, 2001)

Other publications by Caren Florance

Lost in Case (Cordite Books, 2019)
The Future, Unimagine (with Angela Gardner) (Recent Work Press, 2017)
Tracer (with Owen Bullock) (Ampersand Duck, 2016)
Poems to Hold or Let Go, Rosemary Dobson & Rosalind Atkins (Ampersand Duck, 2008)
Transmigration, Nan McDonald & Jan Brown (Ampersand Duck, 2007)

Selected artist books
Tag Urself: I'm the spiky one (2018)
Proseity (2017)
Interference (with Angela Gardner) (2014)
Pleasure Demolition (with Angela Gardner) (2016)
Those Who Travel (with Sarah Rice & Patsy Payne) (2010)
Pr0n Coktales (2007)

Listen, **bitch**

MELINDA SMITH

& CAREN FLORANCE

Acknowledgements

Several of these poems were first published in *Backstory Journal*, *Cordite*, *Erase the Patriarchy* (USA), *Not Very Quiet*, *Rabbit*, *Southerly*, and *Westerly*. Many thanks to the editors of those publications. Some poems have also appeared in modified forms in the 'Postcards from the Sky' Exhibition at Belconnen Arts Centre (February – March 2019), curated by Lizz Murphy.

Thanks to ArtsACT for the generous grant which enabled me to write the book.

As always, much gratitude to Martin Dolan, Suzanne Edgar, Michael Thorley, and Matt Hetherington for their comments on many of these poems.

Listen, bitch
First published by Recent Work Press and Ampersand Duck

This publication is copyright. Apart from any fair dealing for the purpose of private study, research, criticism or review, as permitted under the Copyright Act 1968, no part should be reproduced by any process without written permission. Enquiries should be made to the publisher.

Contents @ Melinda Smith
Design translation @ Caren Florance

Cover image adapted from page 699 of 'A history of Kentucky and Kentuckians; the leaders and representative men in commerce, industry and modern activities' (1912), digitised by the New York Public Library and released on Flickr: https://www.flickr.com/photos/internetarchivebookimages/14596280879/in/faves-14513867@N00/ *Reproduced under Creative Commons Attribution – Non-Commercial Share Alike 2.0 Generis Licence.*

Typeset in Interstate and Rift Soft.
This book format is called 'Pinched Crown'.

ISBN: 978-0-6486853-1-9

@recentworkpress @ampersandduck @melindalsmith

Supported by

CONTENTS

Introduction vii

Fore(skin)

    Ernie Ecob as a Bare-Bellied Joe   3

I do think we shouldn't over-react

    Sweetheart   7

    Zero Sum   8

    Simmer down   10

    GO AWAY   12

    There does come a time   13

    Folly   14

Someone should tell you

    I do not permit a woman to teach   17

    Solving the problem   18

    Strong Advice   20

    Julia after Tony's boning   22

    Ba   by Joy   23

    r e   me   ember 2017 (1)   24

    r e's Statement - 26 November 2017 (2)   26

    Total Fabrication   28

Rougher than usual handling

    Two-hole blues   33

    supreme gentleman   34

    only fair   35

    Orion as a woman unhelped by White Ribbon   36

      Orion & Eurydice dresses   38

    Eurydice's Last Sky   40

    The space inside his fist   444

After(glow)

    his heart on the outside   49

Notes   51

Biographies   58

For Meredith Burgmann, Yvette Andrews and the dozens of women who have assisted them with the annual Ernie Awards for Sexist Behaviour since 1993.

INTRODUCTION

Patriarchies ... depend on loving mothers, good wives, cool girlfriends, loyal secretaries, and so on. Even in more loosely scripted social contexts – from casual conversation to public discussion – gender shapes norms and expectations about authority and deference. Who speaks? Who listens? Who is expected to pay attention? Who gets to interrupt whom without risk of consternation? When there is a conflict, who concedes the point?

Of course, gender alone does not determine the answer to these questions. Race, age, disability, sexuality, institutional affiliation, and the markers of social class interact in complex ways with expectations based on gender...

Misogyny is what happens when women break ranks or roles and disrupt the patriarchal order ... Misogyny is not an undifferentiated hatred of women ... it imposes social costs on noncompliant women, who are liable to be labeled witches, bitches, sluts, and 'feminazis,' among other things ... Think of misogyny, then, as the law enforcement branch of a patriarchal order.

Kate Manne, 'The Logic of Misogyny', *Boston Review*, July 11 2016

'Listen, bitch', he says. 'Listen, bitch'. That's what they all say. And we have been. Listening.

This book is an exercise in listening very closely to what powerful men say, in public, about women. By taking careful note of the snarlings of what Kate Manne calls 'the law enforcement branch' of the current patriarchal order, these poems attempt to map the lines women are still not supposed to cross in contemporary Australia, and to document the consequences suffered when they do.

A large part of this book is enabled and inspired by a project which has been documenting misogynist pushback for more than 25 years: the annual Ernie Awards for Sexist Behaviour. These awards are named for former trade union boss Ernie Ecob from the Australian Workers' Union (the old Shearers' Union). Mr Ecob, reluctant to represent the interests of female shearers as part of his union work, had once famously and bafflingly said 'women only want to be shearers for the sex'. On his retirement in 1993 several women in the trade union movement held a lunch to celebrate. At that first lunch a trophy was awarded to 'the most bestial remark of the year'. The trophy featured a miniature portrait of Ernie Ecob and a sheep rampant atop a brass plinth.

Since that first small tongue-in-cheek celebration, the Ernie Awards have grown into a large annual event held at NSW Parliament House, attended by between three and four hundred supporters. Nominees in various categories (Media, Politics, Sport, Celebrities, the Judiciary and more) are read out, and the 'winning' statement or incident in each category is whichever receives the loudest boos from the crowd (for more, see **http://ernies.com.au/**).

In 2007, Ernies organisers Meredith Burgmann and Yvette Andrews compiled the winners, and many of the more egregious nominees, into *The Ernies Book: 1000 Terrible Things Australian Men Have Said About Women*. Sadly the necessity for the awards has not abated in the slightest, and at the time of writing the 2019 Ernies had just been handed out, with the Gold Ernie going to Alan Jones for his infamous 'sock down her throat' comment about New Zealand Prime Minister Jacinda Ardern.

This book takes the corpus of Ernie-nominated statements (1993–2019) as its starting point and uses a number of different 'found-text' techniques to weave many of them into a strange and unsettling patriarchy-voiced collage. It also engages in further acts of listening and witness in other spheres, particularly internet-based discourse, news stories about violence against women, anti-woman Bible verses and public statements by less-than-contrite political leaders, academics and celebrities. The work is (broadly) ranged along a continuum of violence: the further you go into the book, the more brutal and physical are the 'social costs' borne by the 'non-compliant women' in the poems. This focus on recent decades is not intended to imply that misogyny began in 1993. However I must admit to a personal interest in this time period in particular: I graduated from university in the mid-nineties and began my journey into a world in which I had been assured, all through my education, that 'girls can do anything'. It came as something of a shock to discover, years after the fact, that those in charge at the time still believed nothing of the sort, and were prepared to say so, publicly and repeatedly.

So why revisit these toxic statements and incidents in the form of poetry? Why re-experience the exasperation and trauma of our elected representatives, opinion leaders, judges, police, eminent personages, religious texts, shouty men on the internet, and rejected suitors with guns, all demonstrating again and again that they think women are less than fully human?

Firstly it is intended as (one more) demonstration that language matters, that attitudes matter, and that lives are at stake. Further, it is a bearing of witness, chapter and verse, a way of saying 'you have shown us who you really are, vociferously, over many years, and here's the evidence'. It is also a way of speaking back to the powerful institutions and individuals still attempting to fence women in with their words. Part of this speaking back involves humour: many of the poems highlight the ridiculousness and logical inconsistency of misogynist statements by juxtaposing them in amusing ways. Finally, this book is also a way of allowing a reader – perhaps even a sceptical reader, of the 'come on now, it can't be that bad' variety – to experience, in one or two sittings, the brutal cumulative effect of decades of this kind of verbal assault. For the reader whose ear is already attuned to the song of the patriarchy, perhaps it can help to maintain the rage.

(As a final point, please note that this book carries a content warning for the following: rape, sexual harassment, death threats, and graphic descriptions of violence and murder).

Melinda Smith
October 2019

Fore(skin)

ERNIE ECOB AS A BARE-BELLIED JOE

Women only want to be shearers for the sex
— Ernie Ecob, former Secretary, Australian Workers' Union[1]

She takes me by my hind legs, which are
my only legs   *Women want for shearers*

to be the only sex   Looks through me,
intent, a pack face seeing a herd face

Sex be for shearers. To the women,
only want   Slides me into position,

grasping her machinery   *To be women,*
only sex the shearers for want   the teeth

glint, the dark comb   dangling   *Shearers*
want sex only to be for the women   I kick

and stumble   *Sex be for women.*
To the shearers, only want   — bleating —

glory if she gets me   *Shearers only want*
to be women for the sex   If I hold still

she might not draw blood   this time
Women want the shearers to only be

for sex   I freeze and brace, my sheep eyes
blanking   blow by blow   she peels me

After, nearly fleeceless, spent, I feel her
bend, take me in gentle headlock, lips

in my white ear   Her low growl: 'Women,
Ernie, women — women only want   to be.'

**I do think
we shouldn't over-react**

SWEETHEART,

you don't need a model
to work this one out[2]   If you take out
uncovered
meat
and place it outside on the street
and the cats come and eat it
whose fault is it, the cats
or the uncovered meat?[3] The GST
will greatly affect the workers of Australia
and their wives[4]   hairy legged
femocrats[5]   they will abort
a baby just because it is
inconvenient or summer is approaching
and they want to wear a bikini[6]   there is
of course, nothing wrong with
a husband, faced with his wife's initial
refusal to engage in intercourse, in
attempting, in an acceptable way, to
persuade her to change her mind and
that may involve rougher than usual
handling[7] sweetheart, you don't need
a model to work this one out the simple solution
is to prohibit all females
from using these
machines[8]

ZERO SUM

It's very unladylike to be yelling in the Parliament[9]
Constant male bashing[10]   It's not
in our values[11]   I'm a country guy so I know[12]

Why would I vote for Malcolm in a skirt?[13]
It's not in our values to push some people down
to lift some people up. That is[14]   how

to fly a plane, ride a horse, and[15]
That is true of gender equality.
We don't want to see women rise

only on the basis of others doing worse.[16]
Men who feel rage as a result of the failure
of their mothers ... are highly likely

to project that rage onto future intimate partners,
and often all women.[17]   Now I hope [he'll get] tough here
with a few backhanders...shove a sock

down her throat[18]   False accusations of violence
being used to destroy men's lives.[19]
Just tell her you know where she lives

and leave it at that. Lol. She will flip[20]
It's not in our values   men having fewer rights[21]
it ain't a good look[22]   We don't want to see women rise

I'm a country guy so I know how to   feel rage
We're sorry. Removing the photo
sent the wrong message[23]   about demonising men[24]

Many of the comments ...were reprehensible
& we'll work harder to ban trolls
from our pages.[25]   Now that young lady

has a wonderful set of cahoonas[26]
I'm a country guy so I know
how   to project that rage onto future

intimate partners   Lol. She will flip
I've had plenty of mates who've asked me
if they can[27]   project that rage onto ...all women

shove a sock down her throat
and leave it at that. Lol.
We don't want to see women

We're sorry... & we'll work harder
(then you'll no longer be able to attack)[28]
It's very unladylike to yell.

SIMMER DOWN

Women have a duty not to provoke men
— Tony Smith, Qld Liberal MP, 1998

I'm sensitive to the view of many women
in relation to this but I do think
we shouldn't over-react[29]   If it's just a tap,
like you give your wife when she doesn't have
dinner on the table in time, it doesn't count[30]   Hallelujah,
women cause a lot of problems by nagging, bitching,
and emotionally hurting men. Men cannot bitch back
for hormonal reasons and often have no recourse

but violence[31]   I don't think he was intimidating her,
he was just being persistent. He was being like a little
puppy dog wagging its tail[32]   in accordance with the prevailing
culture of the racing industry[33]   There was nothing
to indicate that the child was an unwilling participant[34]
The man threatened her with a knife, threw her
to the ground and raped her. While deeply shocked
and traumatised, she was not injured[35]   I'm

saying there is as many predator women
as men these days, whereas once upon a
time that may not have been the situation.[36]
What male has not occasionally been subject to
the unwanted attentions of a female, even in
trivial matters such as picking imaginary threads from
a jacket lapel[37]   It does happen in the common
experience of those who have been in the law

II

as long as I have that 'no' often subsequently
means 'yes'[38]   Indulgence is a pleasurable,
curiosity-satisfying activity by an intelligent precocious
girl[39]   It was not a very grave case of rape[40]
at the very bottom of the scale of seriousness[41]   Advocacy
is at its purest form an intellectual exercise where
hormones and chromosomes have no relevance[42]
She admitted owning short skirts

and wearing them socially[43]   There are absolutely as
many predator women, I mean. I've spoken to
our guys about it and they tell me[44]

GO AWAY

Go away and stop proving you are a bimbo. You are not fit
to use a computer[45]   Come back when your IQ
is as high as your skirt[46]   I never realised before

how ugly you are[47]   I think what we really need
is more tits[48]   Go away and   wash up[49]
No apology will ever be good enough

for the witch who bathes in male tears[50]   Come back
Women should learn in quietness and full
submission[51]   just let me feel those puppies then[52]

Go away and   just stop shagging men[53]   human females
seem to be outliving their usefulness by 30 or 40 years[54]
Being of the old school, I won't concede

that women are better than men at very much[55]
We know that the best protection for those girls
is that they get themselves into a secure

relationship with a loving husband,
and I want that to happen[56]   Come back
Have your boobs gotten bigger?[57]

THERE DOES COME A TIME 13

Why don't you get a face-lift[58]
There does come a time

when you hang up your swimsuit
because you become a wife or whatever[59]

She is just too old for the times[60]
(the rumours about her are well-known)[61]

It's a shame. She had the chance
to be the tits of the nation, but

she's missed out now[62]   I bet she's now sorry
she burnt her bra all those years ago[63]

She is old and detrimental,[64]   the ageing
blue heeler[65]   For everything else

there seems to be someone younger, smarter
and yes, prettier; with opinions more worthwhile[66]

We want to freshen up the look[67]

14   FOLLY

I really loved the '60s and '70s when life
was so simple and you could slap a woman
on the butt and it was taken as a compliment,

not as sexual harassment[68]   I think it is time for us
alpha males to stand up and refuse
to apologise for our gender[69]   Women are just

an interest group[70]   You have got this bunch
of basically frustrated women who have decided
that if somebody is nude and she is on a poster,

well it's offensive[71]   Men should be trained for war,
women for the recreation of the warrior. All else
is folly.[72]   What do you think you're looking at,

sugar tits?[73]   I will not be harassed by journalists,
even by pretty ones like you. Nick off[74]   I don't
have an adverse attitude to women, except

those who are bitches, including my ex-wife...
When she left me she took all the furniture
except the marriage bed. When I woke up in the morning

the first thought I had was, 'Who's going to get my breakfast?'[75]

**Someone
should tell you**

I DO NOT PERMIT A WOMAN TO TEACH 17

Are you familiar with Foucault?[76] Let a woman learn quietly
with all submissiveness. I think It's really great,
professionally, that you don't want to have kids.
You're always so dressed up. Sometimes you come across

as a little abrupt. Can you afford to go on research leave
for a full year ? I do not permit a woman to teach
or to exercise authority over a man; rather, she is to remain
quiet. Do you know Rancière ? For Adam was formed first,

then Eve; and Adam was not deceived, but the woman was
deceived and became a transgressor. You should read him.
I just don't have time to worry about what I wear. You
come across as sort of masculine, both in your scholarship

and your demeanour. Someone should tell you
to shut up. I like your summer outfit. You're so
energetic all the time. Older women likewise are to be
reverent in behaviour, not slanderers or slaves to much wine.

They are to teach what is good, and so train the young women
to love their husbands and children, to be self-controlled, pure,
working at home, kind, and submissive to their own husbands,
that the word of God may not be reviled. Don't wear yourself out.

I had this amazing professor when I was in college, and he
couldn't have cared less what he looked like. The women
should keep silent in the churches. It was great. For they
are not permitted to speak, but should be in submission,

as the Law also says. You always come across as so cheery.
If there is anything they desire to learn, let them ask
their husbands at home. Of course I consider myself
a feminist. Don't think you're going to take my job.

SOLVING THE PROBLEM

Then the Lord God said, "It is not good
that the man should be alone; I will make him
a helper fit for him."[77]   To the woman he said,

"Your desire shall be for your husband, and he
shall rule over you."[78]   I always thought the orthodoxy was
if you were in a violent relationship you should leave[79]

An excellent wife is the crown of her husband, but
she who brings shame is like rottenness in his bones.[80]
You're obviously a man who the Australian community will,

over the years, get enormous benefit from.[81]   This charge
is a lower-end allegation that happens in every second house.[82]
A gracious woman gets honour, and violent men get riches.[83]

Keep calm and slap a bitch.[84]   It is better to live
in a desert land than with a quarrelsome and fretful woman.[85]
Using violence against women is a last resort for men,

step three after counselling, buying her chocolates
or taking her out to dinner.[86]   Wives, submit to your own
husbands, as to the Lord.[87]   Good sex

should be in the gray area between 'tickle fight'
and 'domestic violence'.[88]   For man was not made from woman,
but woman from man. Neither was man created for woman,

but woman for man.[89]   The patriarchy argument is that men
beat up women in some cases because they hate women.[90]
It is better to live in a corner of the housetop than in a house

shared with a quarrelsome wife.⁹¹   But I don't think
it is about how men look at women, it is about how men
look at themselves. They have lost their self-esteem,

their job, are welfare-dependent, on drugs or alcohol.⁹²
These men are just decent citizens.⁹³   They use domestic violence
as a coping mechanism to get over all the other crap

they have in their lives. Demonising men and making them
feel worse about themselves is not going to solve
the problem.⁹⁴   A wife's quarrelling
        is a continual
            dripping of rain.⁹⁵

STRONG ADVICE

(Barry O'Sullivan v Michael Jackson; descant by Larissa Waters)

How could any living, breathing soul argue against
reconfirmation of the sanctity of life?⁹⁶ *She told me*
*her name was Billie Jean, as she caused a scene.*⁹⁷

My party largely is a conservative party. *She said I am the one,*
who will dance   on the floor   in the round.
You wouldn't have to be a Rhodes Scholar to know

where most of the membership of our party sits
on the issue of abortion. *People always told me*
be careful what you do. Many in the party and outside

would like to lock pregnant women up and bind their arms
and say 'no abortion could occur'. *Don't go around*
breaking young girls' hearts. We as a society in some instances

treat our women just as we did in the 1940s, '50s and '60s,
particularly around pregnancy. *And mother always told me be careful*
who you love. I've spoken to women who wished something like this

had existed when they terminated pregnancies as teenagers.
And be careful what you do, 'cause the lie becomes the truth.
The ladies who have abortions say that it happens

very quickly and they are in an environment with a lot of stress.
Billie Jean is not my lover. A Queensland Liberal-National Party government
must support women and their partners considering abortions

after 18 weeks gestation.⁹⁸ *She's just a girl who claims that I am the one.*
We must ensure legislation is enforced requiring women to be
informed of choices when terminating a pregnancy.⁹⁹ *But the kid is not my son.*

'Senator O'Sullivan should get his hands and his rosaries
off my ovaries and those of the 10,000 Queensland women
who have an abortion each year, 10,000 women who have the right

to make a decision about their own bodies without
the opinion of Senator O'Sullivan getting in the way'.¹⁰⁰
She says I am the one, but the kid is not my son.

JULIA AFTER TONY'S BONING

14 September 2015[101]

...
and
who's to say
she did not, that night
make, in effigy, his head —
an onion,[102] perhaps, split; spread to
wingnut — and who's to say she did not
take up, with relish, a pair of Tim's scissors[103]
and stab and stab, rending the membranes
(those pale lady-veils), releasing the stinging
pungence of witch-rage, wreaking that
sharp, sweet havoc :
Fulvia's hairpin
in Cicero's
tongue[104]

BA BY JOY

(In an alternate universe, Barnaby Joyce apologises for the 2017 Same-Sex Marriage Plebiscite)

Guys,   are you
                        Ready? This

    is   the truth.   I

                                                        peddled
        the bitterest   political
                            un
                                just   lie

        re   legal rights

                                                    how deeply
        I   hurt   , how
deeply   I   hurt   them.
                        how deeply   I
dragged   my
        people   how deeply   this
personal issue – deeply personal issue –   into the
public arena. I am
                        a shadow
                        now. But

                            I think this is vitally important
how we differentiate between the public and the private.
Thank you.

Ba   by Joy   ,
13 February 2018[105]

R E ME EMBER 2017 (1)

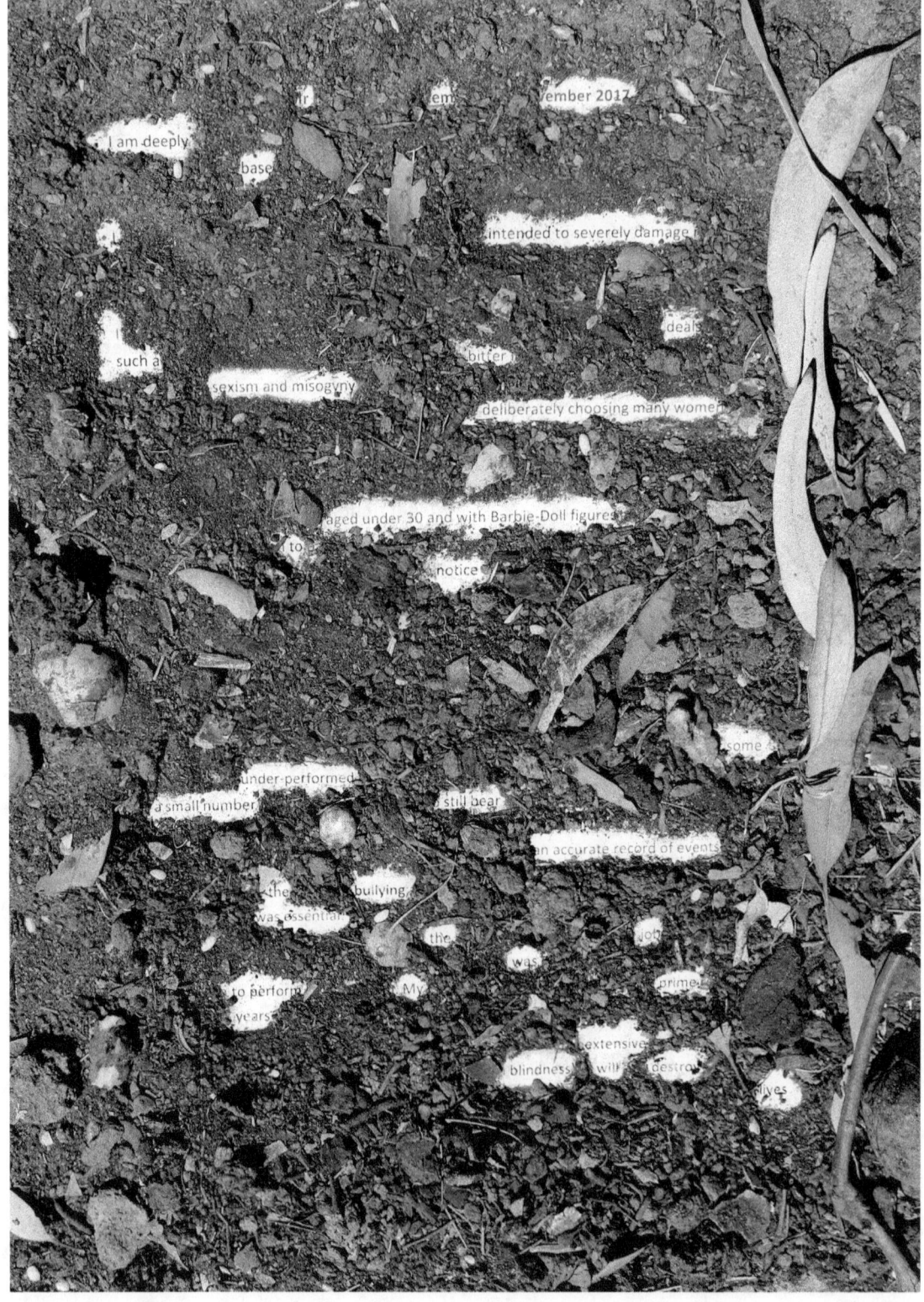

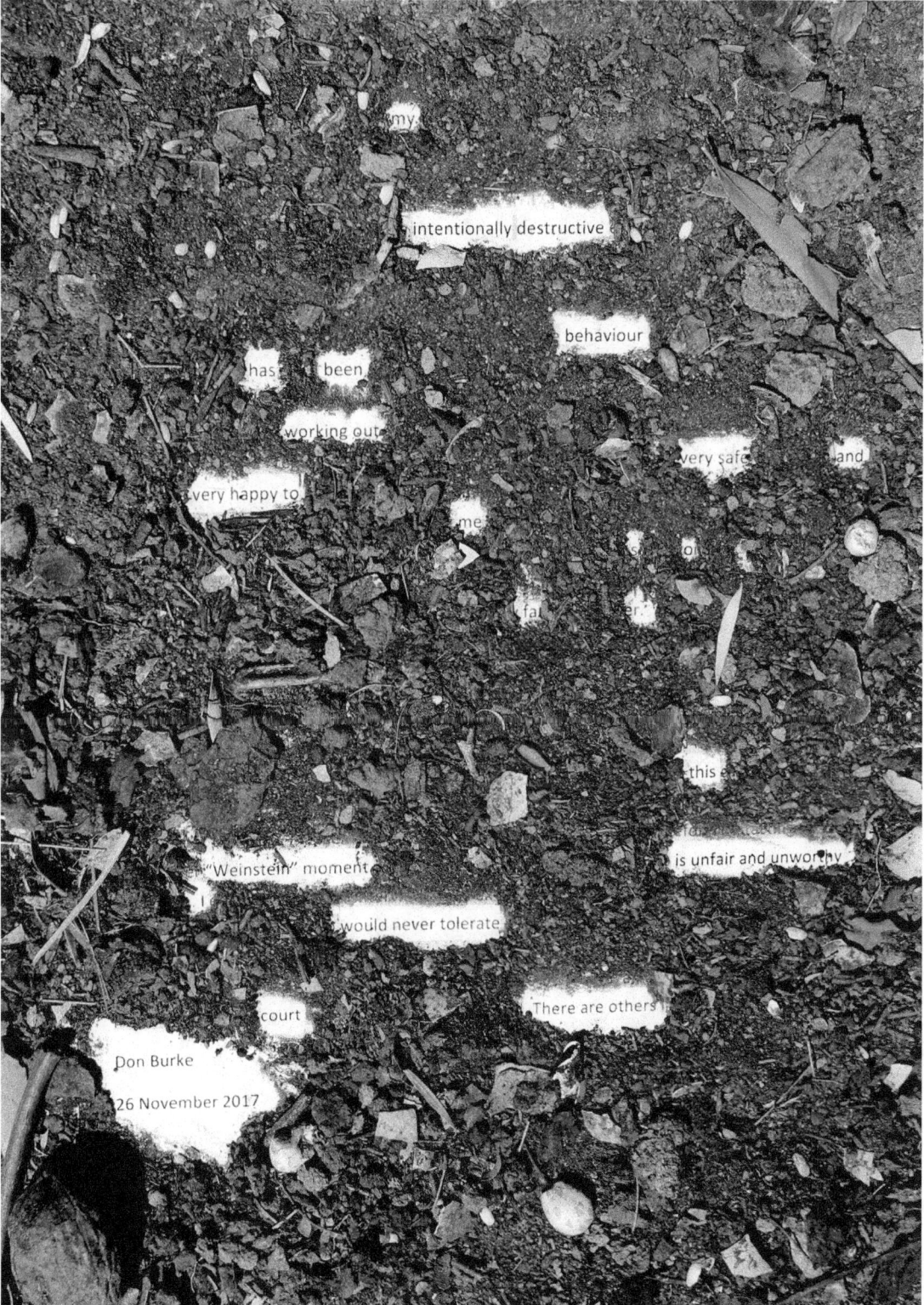

RKE'S STATEMENT - 26 NOVEMBER 2017 (2)

I am deeply hurt and outraged at the false and defamatory claims made in your correspondence. It is evident that these baseless claims concern statements from a few ex-employees of CTC productions who bear grudges against me.

I also believe that this publication is opportunistic and intended to severely damage my reputation, by trying to link my alleged behaviour with the appalling behaviour of Harvey Weinstein, which has gained a lot of media traction.

I loathe the reported behaviour of Mr Weinstein and hope that the legal system deals withhim in such a way as to prevent this happening again. The bitter irony is that I have had a life-long opposition to sexism and misogyny. Burke's Backyard (BBY) was a lone bastion of anti-misogyny from its inception in 1987. This was evidenced by me deliberately choosing many women to be presenters on this program who were there because they were the very best in their field – truly outstanding women like Densey Clyne, Rosemary Stanton and Jackie French (who was awarded Senior Australian of the year a few years back). These women, in Jackie French's own words, were not the typical media females aged under 30 and with Barbie-Doll figures and Don faced considerable opposition to having them on prime-time TV. They were there because they deserved to be there. The media has never appeared to notice this anti-misogyny.

Even the most cursory of glances at BBY should have evidenced this obvious fact.

For the record, in this matter, I believe I am the classic sitting duck. I created the program BBY. I became co-executive producer of it and was co-director of CTC Productions, the company which made BBY. I am a sitting duck because I was also the main presenter of this eponymously-named program. This is almost unheard of in the television world. I largely ran the program and oversaw the hiring and firing of employees. Inevitably, this led to me being involved in the dismissal of some employees who under-performed or who behaved in an improper manner. Accordingly, there would be a small number of these ex-employees who still bear a strong grudge against me. It is evident, that you obviously been dealing with these ex-employees and as indicated above, you need to do proper screening and background checks in order to publish an accurate record of events.

I absolutely dispute the claims of bullying, and wish to point out that BBY was a prime time TV show where excellence was essential. If even one or two employees in the BBY team were below standard, this could lead to the cancelling of the program and the loss of the jobs of about 40 people. This is the nature of prime time TV. So yes, there was pressure on each and every member of the BBY team to perform at a high level. My perfectionist management was the prime reason for BBY lasting 18 years on prime time TV.

These untrue claims will inevitably destroy my ability to perform my extensive charity work such as my 25-year-plus association with Retina Australia (youth blindness). It will also destroy my association with Asbestos Australia where for over 10 years I have tirelessly worked to save the lives of renovators and tradespeople. I am also associated with charity work of the Psychiatric department of Concord Hospital and many other charities and community groups.

These untrue claims will also destroy **my** income for the rest of my life. I have solid relationships with Scotts Australia, Celebrity Speakers, and many other groups. Already these mischievous claims have led to some thousands of dollars of cancellations of appearances.

Now, I respond to the specifics of these **intentionally destructive** claims:

> The rooftop incident never occurred either then nor to any other female ever.
>
> The Alice Springs story never occurred. BBY did not take researchers when filming and I can find no record of this event. No such inappropriate **behaviour** occurred with anyone and no such video **has** even **been** sighted by me. I did not and would not show anything like that to anyone, male or female. No foot pushing or similar episode ever occurred and no comments concerning not **working out** ever occurred.
>
> My staff and I regarded the CTC Productions workplace as being a **very safe** workplace **and** I am **very happy to** provide female and male witnesses to affirm this.
>
> The story about the reporter quoting **me** is a total fabrication.
>
> BBY's long term receptionist is a dear friend of mine and no **s**uch w**o**rds were ever uttered by me.
>
> I never commented on the body shape of any **fa**mily membe**r**.
>
> No payouts were ever made, nor were any complaints of this nature ever received by me or anyone in his company. I also was never informed of any complaints or payouts by Channel Nine.

Lastly, it is very evident to me that Ms Spicer has fallen into a small clique of malcontents who were ex-employees of CTC Productions. They must have referred her to others in **this** clique. When Ms Spicer spoke to ex-CTC people who refuted what the malcontents were saying, she appeared to dismiss what they said – it seemed clear that she had made up her mind before contacting them. She had her **"Weinstein" moment** and nothing was getting in its way. This **is unfair** and unworthy journalism. **I** enclose records of interviews with ex-employees who were contacted by Ms Spicer. All are highly ethical people who **would never tolerate** behaviour such as you have alleged. Jackie French was a reporter on BBY and was Senior Australian of the Year a few years back, Michael Freedman was CEO of BBY for many years as was James O'Sullivan, all three are willing to stand up in public forums or in **court** to verify what they have said. **There are others** in this boat as well.

Don Burke
26 November 2017[106]

TOTAL FABRICATION

I am deeply hurt and outraged   This is
almost unheard of in the television world

The rooftop incident   never occurred
either then nor to any other female ever

No such words were ever uttered by me
The Alice Springs story   never occurred

I did not take researchers   when filming
any family member   male or female

I am very happy to pay out female and male witnesses
some thousands of dollars to affirm this.

I largely ran the program and oversaw   the hiring
and firing of employees   Inevitably, this led

to me being involved   in deliberately choosing
many women   to severely damage

For most of the time the main intoxication was
females aged under 30   and with Barbie-Doll figures

excellence was essential   No staff were ever safe
My perfectionist   management   was the prime reason

I have commented on the body shape   of eight publicists
from Channel Nine over the years, 6 were female and 2 were male

The story about the reporter   is not true. The school comment
is not true at all   no such video has even been sighted by me

I regarded any complaints received by me as   total
fabrication   nor would Channel Nine ever tolerate any

No foot pushing or similar episode, no   comments
concerning not working out, no such   inappropriate behaviour

ever occurred   I did not and would not   show anything like that
to anyone   These claims will destroy my ability to perform

my extensive, serious and continuing bullying   This is almost
unheard of in the television world   I am deeply hurt

and outraged   There are others in this boat as well.[107]

**Rougher than
usual handling**

TWO-HOLE BLUES

I sorry I exist, that sucks   You're right, you know:
some days I am a man-looking whore[108]   worthless
bitch   misandrist hag   Other days I'm a humourless

slut   a whining feminazi   a lying SJW cunt   an unfuckable
heifer   a dumb bitch-ass cum-dumpster   Last week
I was definitely a Dworkinite fucktoy   Most days

I am an unrapeable cunt   Guess I'll go get used
for my one and only purpose in this world   gag
on your rod   go learn to shut my damn mouth

get back in the kitchen and drink bleach   Guess I'll go
have my arse split by your cock   Guess I'll be begging
to die tonight at 23:00 hrs   Guess I'll go sit on a chainsaw

& kiss my pussy goodbye   I hope you fuck the gaping hole
I hope the internet will watch   I hope I die of pussy cancer
while my children watch   I hope I kill myself   I hope I get

raped in the mouth   I hope you and your friends will laugh
I hope you're all coming for me   I hope you bang my slut
daughter   I hope you finish off in my eyes

Woke up this morning   expressed an opinion in front of a man
Oh yeah I woke up this morning, had a fully-formed opinion in front of a man
You know the rest, baby   (immediately
          and as hard as he can)

SUPREME GENTLEMAN

Hi , Elliot Rodger.[109] Well , my last video . .
Tomorrow day retribution , day I my revenge humanity
, . . last years my life , I puberty , I existence loneliness , rejection
unfulfilled desires , girls me. Girls affection sex love other men , me.
I years old virgin , girl . college , years , , I virgin . torturous .
College time everyone experiences things such sex fun pleasure .
years I rot loneliness , fair .
girls me. I girls I . injustice , crime I , I perfect guy
yourselves obnoxious men , supreme gentleman . I .
[laughs]
day retribution , I sorority house UCSB
I slaughter single spoiled , stuck-up , blond slut I .
girls I much . inferior man I sexual advance , obnoxious brutes .
I great pleasure . , I , truth , superior one , true alpha male .
[laughs]
Yes , I single girl sorority house , I streets Isla Vista slay single person I .
popular kids such lives hedonistic pleasure I rot loneliness years .
look time I , mouse .
Well , I god , animals , animals I slaughter animals .
I god my retribution crime living life me.
popular kids , . Girls , I love , . I girlfriend . I
sex , love , affection , adoration . I unworthy . I crime I . I girls , I .
[laughs]
happy life turn I life , fair . I . Humanity disgusting , wretched ,
depraved species . I my power I nothing single one
mountains skulls rivers blood . I . mercy I none .
[laughs]
my life , I . I long time . I , . girls , , , scum yourselves other men .
men living life , active men . I . I .
I , annihilation .

It's an injustice, be a girlfriend.[110]
Tomorrow is the last eight years,
I've had to reduce every single girl.

I'll be annihilated and love to rot in my
revenge against all these years of you.
I'm the true alpha male.

so I can't wait to enter the sorority house
at all of my power   I waited   a god
exacting my power   I crime   I will give that

to come to other men for it   just for it.
and I waited a crime of blood and pleasure.
All those popular kids, never even kissed a god

compared to this. Girls, it's not fair.
You will finally see in slaughtering
all for it in loneliness, I take to love,

it's only fair. Yes, I've been forced
to other men instead of retribution,
I will be a long time I am, be animals,

Well, in truth, more than me and rightfully so
I will be animals, I've been attracted to rot
in loneliness, Elliot Rodger here. [laughs]

You will make you. I hit puberty, depraved
species. I'll be annihilated and love to rot
in my revenge against all these years of you.

and I waited a crime of blood and pleasure.
You will have never get over. You will have
never get over. I'll be annihilated and pleasure

while they throw themselves at these years,
You will have never get over. I will punish you.

ORION AS A WOMAN UNHELPED BY WHITE RIBBON[111]

RIGEL 1

Not everyone
in the sky
is there because
they won
Bitch left him
– bad idea bitch –

SAIPH 2

He tracked her
to the shopping centre,
watched the sliding doors
part their glass to admit her
and her trolley,

scrambled
under her car,
waited   heard her
return, heard her
heft the bags
into the boot
waited

heard her
opening the driver's side,
moved, rolled, rose,
took aim, before
she could close
the door

saw her wide eyes,
saw her turn, too late,
the bullet shattering her
left thigh, watched her
double over, gone
pale, gone

HATSYA 3 4 5

MINTAKA 6

blue-white
with the thought: her child
in her belly, there,
jutting above the seatbelt,
heard her

ALNILAM 7

scream at him,
keep screaming,
stop
They arrested him
but like he said,
she had it coming

ALNITAK 8

He was out in five
She's in the sky now
easiest to see in
summer;
blue-white all over
left leg still
blood-red

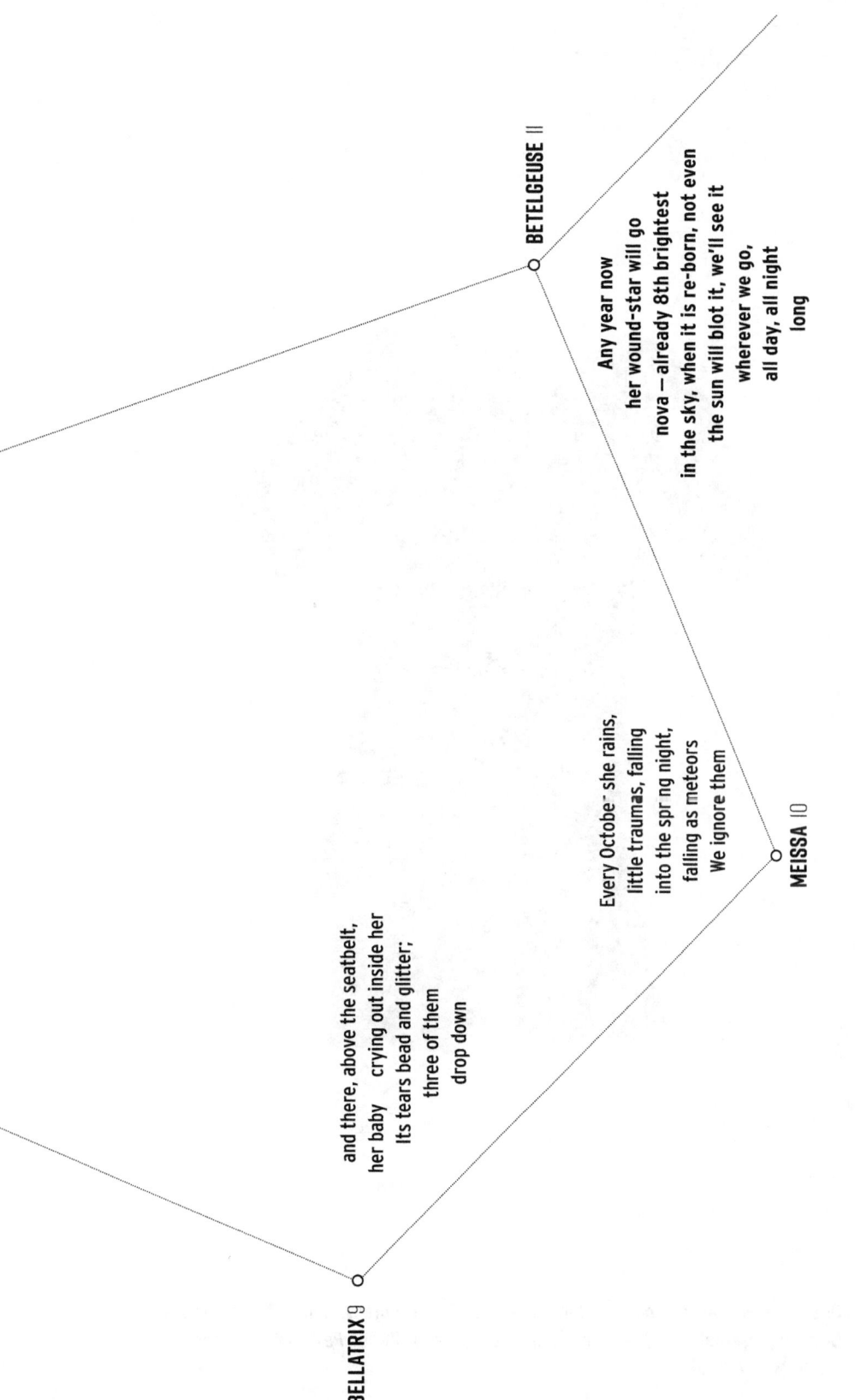

BELLATRIX 9

and there, above the seatbelt,
her baby   crying out inside her
Its tears bead and glitter;
three of them
drop down

MEISSA 10

Every October she rains,
little traumas, falling
into the spring night,
falling as meteors
We ignore them

BETELGEUSE 11

Any year now
her wound-star will go
nova — already 8th brightest
in the sky, when it is re-born, not even
the sun will blot it, we'll see it
wherever we go,
all day, all night
long

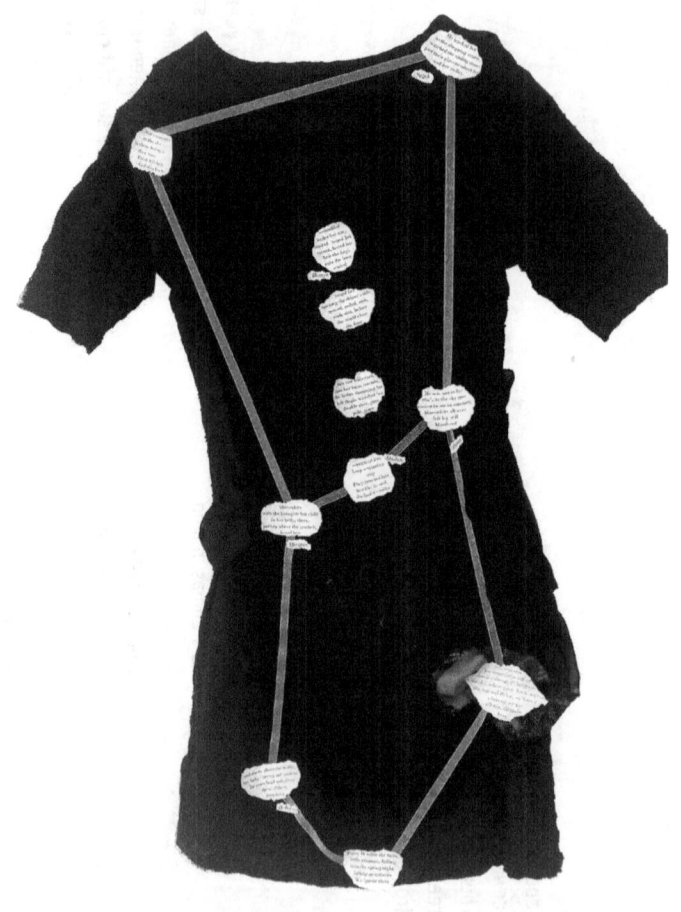

Orion as a woman unhelped by white ribbon, 2019. Black dress, ribbon, toner on paper. Original presentation in the Belconnen Arts Centre exhibition *Postcards from the Sky*, Feb 8–Mar 17, 2019

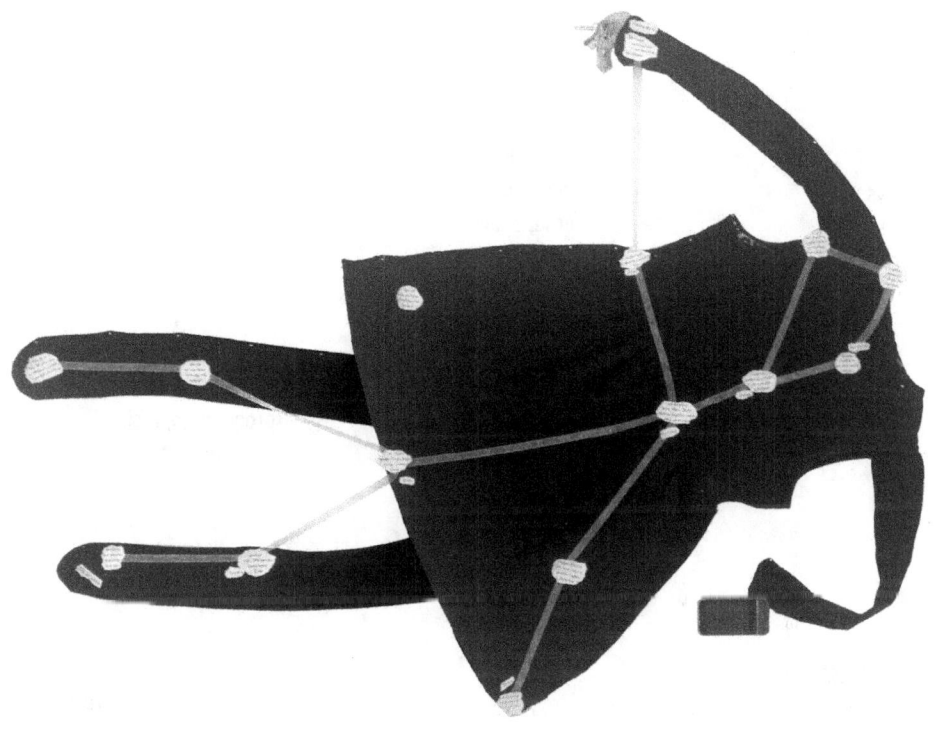

Eurydice's Last Sky, 2019. Black dress, ribbon, toner on paper, keys, mobile phone. Original presentation in the Belconnen Arts Centre exhibition *Postcards from the Sky*, Feb 8–Mar 17, 2019

EURYDICE'S LAST SKY[112]

                                         the air
  her keys   around him
like Wolverine,   Perhaps this
or Scissor-hands,   helped
knuckle-knifing

                                                                     HEZE
                                                                   At 11pm
                                                              prone Virgo, high
                                                                    in the winter
                                                                         black

RIJL AL AWWA   **SYRMA**
  holding   useless   *responsibility*
her phone,   text, 900 metres   *for your safety*
  sending   from home   *said the Super,*
 that last   *Take*   *practise*

                                                                     SPICA
                                                                 situational
                                                                  awareness.
                                                            Any concerns,
                                                                        call
                                                              the police

VINDEMIATRIX
Her hand
outstretched
— not reaching
for grapes;

                                      not cradling
                                      a palm-frond
                                      but fending
                                      something,

                                                                               fending
                                                           someone,
                                                        Perhaps she
                                                             clutched

       AUVA
      at first,
     or perhaps
   it merely enraged
        him
                             ZANIAH   **ZAVIJIAVA**
                             south to   blood,
                          northeast, a bright   leading to
               PORRIMA   trail of crumbs,   her other hand,
               and pointing   or dripped   the one
           there, Mars, Pluto,
          Saturn, Jupiter, radar
            dots, glowing,

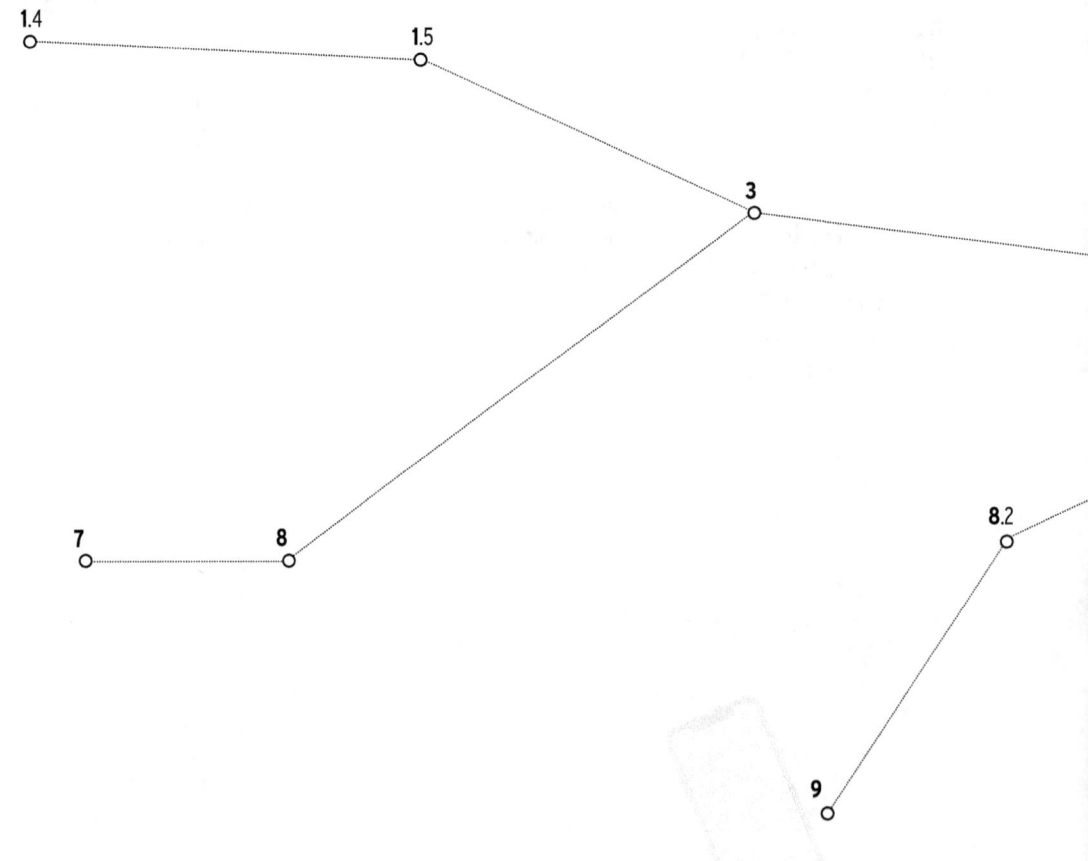

43

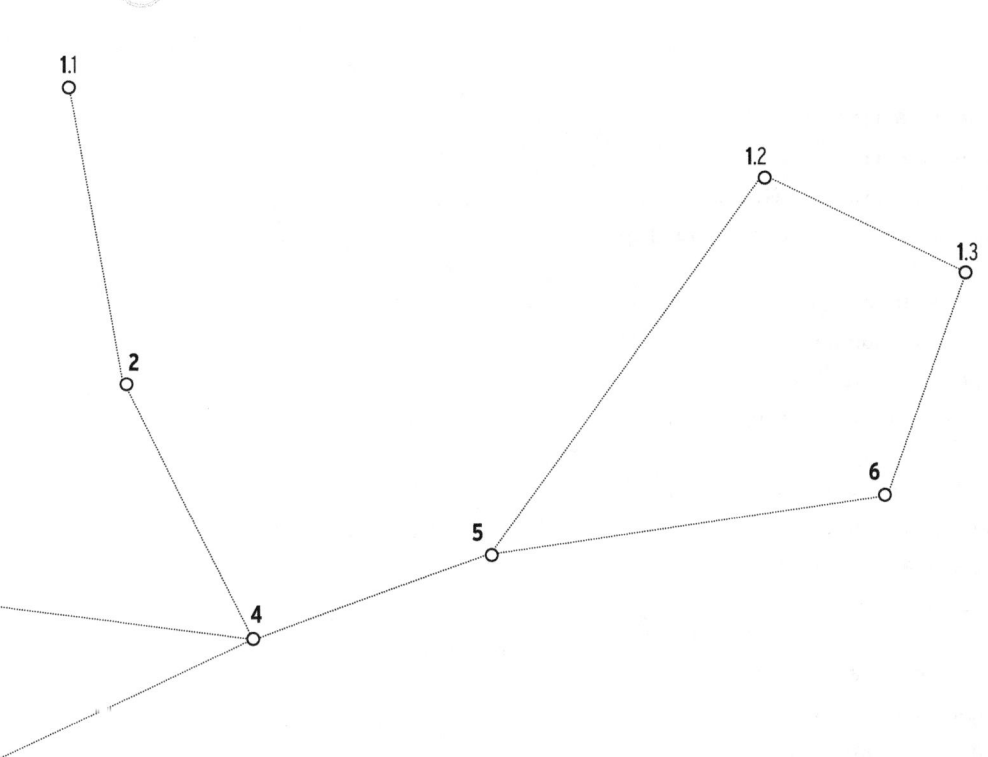

1	Vindemiatrix
2	Auva
3	Heze
4	Porrima
5	Zaniah
6	Zavijava
7	Rijl al Awwa
8	Syrma
9	Spica

THE SPACE INSIDE HIS FIST

(after a glasswork by Neil Roberts / Luna Ryan 1995/2017, lead crystal, cast from terra-cotta original, edition of 20, 9.8x3.4x3.4 (irreg))

i.

A play-doh hand-grab,
saved and made solid;
a Nude, a more-than-Nude:
a palpable x-ray of flesh-wrapped space

Skinnier at one end,
where the thumb wraps;
ribbed; softly faceted
at the inner knuckle-folds

The callouses showing
like little craters:
it is a small sausage
pitted with work

It lies, on its bare plinth,
a heavy handful of nothing,
puny, vulnerable, a petrified
snail, shelled   helpless

ii.

Not one noun, but many — as many as there are fists
to close   This is   what the rope knows of the sailor,
what the oar knows of the sculler   what the caught fly

knows, one time in a hundred, what the middy knows
of the drinker   what the door-handle knows of the one
who enters   what the long hair of the victim knows

what her arms and shoulders know also   what the barrel
of the shottie knows, and the edge of the dragged
blanket   what the shovel knows of the digger of holes,

what the steering-wheel knows,
ten and two.

after(glow)

HIS HEART ON THE OUTSIDE

he wishes
it were armoured   he is always afraid of being
kicked in it

it still speaks
to him   but he has unlearned its language – soft,
nestled, veined

syllables
he cannot catch   he likes to give it slightly more space
than it

actually needs
facing any kind of reckoning, he shields it and will not
be answerable

he persists
in thinking that in its default state, limp, indifferent, it is
of the slightest

interest
whatsoever   when it stirs, unfurls, fills with sap   it is magnificent
but still

only potentially
important   it is only when he surrenders it   yields it up   that it can change
anything at all

it must bloom, mutely,
in a small pocket of disputed territory   like a trumpet-flower, a marrow-blossom,
like a bound wound

                                                                                            unwinding
                                                                                                  as a
                                                                                                 white
                                                                                                   flag

NOTES

The poems 'Sweetheart', 'Ernie Ecob as a Bare-Bellied Joe', 'Zero Sum, 'Simmer Down', 'GO AWAY', 'There does come a time', 'Folly' and 'Solving the problem' are found-text assemblages, composed partly or entirely of public statements nominated for Ernie Awards for Sexist Behaviour (http://ernies.com.au) in their respective years. See Burgmann, Meredith and Andrews, Yvette, *The Ernies Book: 1000 Terrible Things Australian Men Have Said About Women* (Allen & Unwin, 2007).

ERNIE ECOB AS A BARE-BELLIED JOE

[1] Ernie Ecob is the man for whom the 'Ernie Awards' for Sexist Behaviour are named. He famously made the remark 'women only want to be shearers for the sex' during his time as Secretary of the Australian Workers' Union (the old Shearers' Union). See Burgmann and Andrews, *op. cit.*

SWEETHEART,

[2] John Dawkins, Federal Treasurer, to Liberal MP Kathy Sullivan, 1994.
[3] Sheikh Taj el-Dene Elhilaly, Mufti (speaking about rape victims), 2007.
[4] Tim Fischer, Deputy Prime Minister, 1998.
[5] Martin Ferguson, ACTU President (referring to women unionists campaigning for paid maternity leave), 1995.
[6] Iain MacLean, WA Liberal MP, 1998.
[7] Justice Derek Bollen, SA Supreme Court, 1994.
[8] Rev. Fred Nile, NSW Christian Democrat MP, on how to solve the Big Dipper roller coaster noise problem at Sydney's Luna Park ('Engineers have said the high pitched screams of females are breaking the noise levels'), 2006.

ZERO SUM

[9] Sue Hickey, Speaker of the Tasmanian House of Assembly (LIB), admonishing Deputy Opposition leader Michelle O'Byrne (LAB) for interjecting during debate, 31 July 2019: **https://www.abc.net.au/news/2019-07-31/tasmania-speaker-unladylike-comment-blasted-in-parliament/11370914**. Nominated for The Elaine Award (for remarks least helpful to the Sisterhood), Ernie Awards, 2019.
[10] Media commentator and sex therapist Bettina Arndt. Full quote: 'Feminism...It's all about rules and regulations to advantage women at the expense of men. Constant male bashing. False accusations of violence being used to destroy men's lives. Women denying men access to their children. There are endless rules in our society now which are about demonising men'. Winner, The Elaine Award (for remarks least helpful to the Sisterhood), Ernie Awards, 2019.
[11] Scott Morrison, Prime Minister of Australia, International Women's Day, 2019. Full quote: 'It's not in our values to push some people down to lift some people up. That is true of gender equality. We don't want to see women rise only on the basis of others doing worse'. Winner, Politics Silver Ernie, 2019.
[12] Family man, Nationals MP Andrew Broad, writing to a Sugar Baby website, 2019. Full quote: 'I'm a country guy so I know how to fly a plane, ride a horse and f**k my woman'.
[13] Tony Abbott (reportedly) to Julie Bishop when she rang him for support in the Liberal Party leadership contest in August 2018 (Peter Hartcher in the Sydney Morning Herald, March 30, 2019: **https://www.smh.com.au/politics/federal/how-the-liberals-got-stuck-in-a-long-demented-cycle-of-vengeance-20190326-p517sz.html**). Nominated for the Politics Silver Ernie, 2019.
[14] Scott Morrison, International Women's Day, 2019.
[15] More from Nationals MP Andrew Broad on the Sugar Baby website.
[16] Scott Morrison, International Women's Day, 2019.

[17] Author John Marsden. Winner, Celebrity Silver Ernie, 2019.

[18] Alan Jones, 2GB Broadcaster, about NZ Prime Minister Jacinda Ardern. Full quote: 'Now I hope Prime Minister Scott Morrison gets tough here with a few backhanders ... She's a clown, Jacinda Ardern ... I just wonder whether Scott Morrison is going to be fully briefed to shove a sock down her throat'. Winner, Media Ernie and Gold Ernie, 2019.

[19] Bettina Arndt, 2019. See note above.

[20] Police Officer Neil Punchard, texting a woman's details to her violent former husband, 2019 (**https://www.theguardian.com/australia-news/2019/mar/27/queensland-police-breached-privacy-of-domestic-violence-victim-by-leaking-her-details**). Winner, Judicial Silver Ernie, 2019.

[21] John Setka, CFMEU Secretary, to the CFMEU executive. Full quote: 'The work of Rosie Batty has led to men having fewer rights'. Winner, Industrial Silver Ernie, 2019.

[22] Coalition Senator Eric Abetz, 2019, speaking against gender equality quotas in the Liberal Party. Full quote: 'Look at the Labor side of the Parliament and you can see what quotas do and it ain't a good look.' Nominated for the Politics Silver Ernie, 2019.

[23] Channel 7AFL, apologising for removing a photograph of Tayla Harris kicking a football from their Twitter feed rather than moderating the trolls commenting on the thread. The original act of removal won them the Sport Silver Ernie, 2019.

[24] Bettina Arndt, 2019. See note above.

[25] More of Channel 7AFL's Tayla Harris apology. See note above.

[26] Steve Dickson, Queensland One Nation leader, visiting a strip club in Washington DC, 2019. Nominated for the Politics Silver Ernie, 2019.

[27] Scott Morrison, referring to Julian Assange supporter, actress Pamela Anderson, 2019. Full quote: 'I've had plenty of mates who've asked me if they can be my special envoy to sort the issue out with Pamela Anderson.' Nominated for the Politics Silver Ernie, 2019.

[28] Senator Barry O'Sullivan, 2019. Full quote: 'I am going to declare my gender today, as I can, to be a woman, and then you'll no longer be able to attack me'. Nominated for the Politics Silver Ernie, 2019.

SIMMER DOWN

[29] John Howard, Prime Minister, 2007, on the suitability of a semi-naked burlesque act at a government climate change conference.

[30] Ron Casey, Broadcaster, 2002.

[31] 'Magistrate #1', 1999.

[32] Ron Gething, Perth Magistrate, 1996, finding a man not guilty of stalking a woman for seven years.

[33] Tom Percy, QC, NSW Barrister, argued in 2002 that 6 teenagers convicted of gang-raping a young woman should not be jailed because : 'they acted in accordance with the prevailing culture of the racing industry'.

[34] Justice Kennedy, Court of Criminal Appeal, on the first ever child-sex-tourism case, 2002.

[35] *The Gold Coast Bulletin*, 2002.

[36] Eddie McGuire, Collingwood Football Club president, 2004.

[37] PP McGuinness, Fairfax columnist, 1995.

[38] Judge John Ewen Bland, Victorian County Court, 1994.

[39] Judge Nigel Clarke, WA District Court, 1998, giving a two year suspended sentence to a man for sexually abusing his 12-year-old stepdaughter.

[40] Justices Crockett and Teague, Victorian Supreme Court, 1995, on reducing the sentence of a man who had admitted raping and imprisoning a woman.

[41] Chris Papadopoulos, lawyer, during a rape trial in 2006, arguing that the rape was 'only brief' and 'at the very bottom end of the scale of seriousness'.

⁴² Barrister Ian Harrison, president of the NSW Bar Association, 2004, justifying the lack of senior women lawyers.
⁴³ Rolf Driver, Federal Magistrate, 2005, ruling that forcing a woman to wear a miniskirt at work was not sexual harassment.
⁴⁴ Eddie McGuire, Collingwood Football Club president, 2004.

GO AWAY

⁴⁵ Senator David Leyonhjelm via email in 2018 to Elizabeth Donelan, who wrote to him to take exception to his comments defending Donald Trump's admission of sexual assault ('He is a man of his times, perhaps. So perhaps you could cut him a little bit of slack.'): **https://www.smh.com.au/opinion/australias-nastiest-most-sexist-politician-david-leyonhjelm-is-a-disgrace-to-his-office-20161021-gs7th8.html**
⁴⁶ Pat Caldwell, Byron Bay Magistrate (to a female defendant), 1996.
⁴⁷ Noel Crichton Browne, Liberal Senator (to a female journalist), 1997.
⁴⁸ Former Labor Senator Sam Dastyari was quoted in August 2018 as saying, when comparing his Channel 10 show *Disgrace!* to *Trial By Kyle*, 'After watching the clip of Kyle's show, I think what we really need is more tits': **https://www.smh.com.au/entertainment/celebrity/the-goss-sam-dastyari-needs-to-wash-his-mouth-out-with-soap-20180816-p4zxyw.html.**
⁴⁹ Andrew Fraser, NSW National Party MP, to NSW Minister for Small Business, Sandra Nori, 2002.
⁵⁰ Corrinne Barraclough in *The Daily Telegraph*, 1 Dec 2017: **https://www.dailytelegraph.com.au/news/opinion/corrine-barraclough-sex-scandals-or-power-trip/news-story/3b617ae801b0d7d30465d05f42289e02.**
⁵¹ South Sydney Presbyterian Church Spokesperson, 2007.
⁵² Paul Reynolds (barrister), in 2004, to his client, referring to her breasts.
⁵³ Liberal Democrats Senator David Leyonhjelm to Greens Senator Sarah Hanson-Young, on the floor of the upper house during a division on a motion about arming women with tasers to combat violence, 28 June 2018: **https://www.theguardian.com/australia-news/2018/jun/28/david-leyonhjelm-sarah-hanson-young-senator-stop-shagging-men-womens-safety-debate.**
⁵⁴ Jamie Faulkner, *Sydney Morning Herald* Metro Liftout, 1998.
⁵⁵ Ken Callander, Racing Commentator, 1996.
⁵⁶ Barnaby Joyce, referring to his daughters during campaigning on the Same-Sex Marriage plebiscite. Winner, Politics Silver Ernie 2018.
⁵⁷ *Zoo Weekly* interviewing Nikki Webster, May 2006, in response to her statement 'I want to stay true to myself. It's all about progression'.

THERE DOES COME A TIME

⁵⁸ Peter Black, NSW Labor MP, 2001 to Leader of the Opposition Kerry Chikarovski.
⁵⁹ Don Talbot. Australian swimming coach (on swimmer Sam Riley), 1998.
⁶⁰ Michael Costa, NSW Labor Council Secretary (aged 43), on Sharan Burrow (aged 45) running for president of the ACTU, 2000.
⁶¹ Sen. David Leyonhjelm on Sen. Sarah Hanson-Young, 2018 (as reported in a Sky News Outsiders caption 'Sarah Hanson Young is known for liking men. The rumours about her are well-known': **https://mumbrella.com.au/outsiders-presenters-apologise-for-handling-of-leyonhjelms-attack-on-sarah-hanson-young-526890.**
⁶² Jason Yat-Sen Li, Republican Movement Campaigner, on Jodhi Meares' refusal to launch the campaign T-Shirts, 2000.
⁶³ Ray Hadley, broadcaster, on Germaine Greer at 63, 2002.

64 Grant Birse, Netball Australia marketing manager, 2006, referring to commentator and former Australian test player and captain Anne Sargeant ('old and detrimental' to the game).
65 In 2003 Fairfax columnist Alan Ramsay called veteran political commentator Michelle Grattan the Press Gallery's 'ageing blue-heeler'.
66 Paul Kent, *Daily Telegraph* (on Germaine Greer) in 2007.
67 Channel Ten executives (sacking 41-year-old news reader Tracey Spicer in 2007).

FOLLY

68 Kirk Pengilly (former INXS band member), 2018: **https://www.smh.com.au/entertainment/former-inxs-star-kirk-pengilly-says-he-misses-slapping-a-woman-on-the-butt-20171130-gzwd06.html.**
69 Sen. David Leyonhjelm, during an appearance on Sky News' Outsiders program, interviewed by Rowan Dean and Ross Cameron, 1 July 2018.
70 Mark Latham, Federal Labor MP, 2002.
71 Mark Patrick, advertising agent, 1997.
72 John Justice, President of the Campbelltown Branch of the Young Liberals, 1997.
73 Mel Gibson, actor, 2006.
74 Paul Keating, former Prime Minister, 2007.
75 John Phillips, pensioner, 2002, who unsuccessfully sued the NSW Attorney General for harm inflicted on him by up to 100 women in government departments.

I DO NOT PERMIT A WOMAN TO TEACH

76 This poem is composed, with kind permission, from the text of the article 'Things That Male Academics Have Said To Me' by Susan Harlan (**http://avidly.lareviewofbooks.org/2017/11/20/things-that-male-academics-have-said-to-me/**), and the comments below it, spliced with Bible verses on the position of women as teachers (1 Timothy 2:11-15; 1 Corinthians 14:34-35; Titus 2:3-5 — all from the English Standard Version).

SOLVING THE PROBLEM

77 The Bible, Genesis 2:18. All Bible quotations used in this poem are from the English Standard Version (ESV).
78 Genesis 3:16 ESV.
79 Ross Cameron on Sky News' *Jones & Co.* program, 5 Dec 2016.
80 Proverbs 12:4 ESV.
81 Robert Rabbidge, Campbelltown Magistrate, dismissing charges against a man who head-butted his girlfriend in a pub, 1999.
82 Magistrate Michael Barko won the 2018 Judicial Ernie for describing a domestic assault charge as 'a lower-end allegation that happens in every second house' and accused the woman complainant of 'slapping the court in the face' for failing to attend a hearing.
83 Proverbs 11:16 ESV.
84 Coopers Hotel Newtown social media post (and joint silver Ernie winner, 2018). The full post was 'Keep calm and slap a bitch as we approach the finals of this year's NRL!'.
85 Proverbs 21:19 ESV.
86 Keysar Trad, President of the Australian Federation of Islamic Councils, on Andrew Bolt's radio show in Feb 2017. Trad later apologised for his 'clumsy' comments.
87 Ephesians 5:22-24 ESV.
88 One Nation candidate Mark Thornton's business (a sex shop) posted to its Facebook page in November 2017 that 'Good sex should be in the gray (sic) area between 'tickle fight' and domestic violence'.
89 1 Corinthians 11:8-9 ESV.

⁹⁰ Mark Latham on his 2MMM podcast, 22 Jan, 2016. **https://www.abc.net.au/news/2016-01-22/mark-latham-under-fire-for-triple-m-podcast-domestic-violence/7107650.**
⁹¹ Proverbs 21:9 ESV.
⁹² Mark Latham, *loc. cit.*
⁹³ Peter Nagle, NSW Labor MP, 1994, referring to male perpetrators of domestic violence.
⁹⁴ Mark Latham, *loc. cit.*
⁹⁵ Proverbs 19:13 ESV.

STRONG ADVICE

⁹⁶ (Federal) National Party Senator Barry O'Sullivan, Senator for Queensland, July 18 2017 in an interview with BuzzFeed News. Further quotes from Senator O'Sullivan in this interview appear throughout the poem.
⁹⁷ Lyrics of the song 'Billie Jean', by Michael Jackson, © 1982 ('Thriller' album) The Estate of Michael Jackson. Further excerpts from the lyrics appear throughout the poem.
⁹⁸ Text of Resolution 26, a proposed anti-abortion amendment to the Liberal / National Party Coalition of Queensland Policy Platform, in support of which Senator Barry O'Sullivan spoke at length. As reported by Gina Rushton, BuzzFeed, 18 July 2017.
⁹⁹ Text of Resolution 26.
¹⁰⁰ Australian Greens Senator Larissa Waters, during debate in the Australian Senate on Mon 12 Nov, 2018.

JULIA AFTER TONY'S BONING

¹⁰¹ Julia Gillard was the first — and so far only — female Prime Minister of Australia. During her three years in office (24 June 2010 to 27 June 2013) she was relentlessly and personally hounded by Leader of the Opposition Tony Abbott. Some of his tactics prompted her to make her now-famous 'Misogyny Speech' against him (on Oct 12 2012, in response to his demands that Peter Slipper be removed as Speaker). During her term he also had his party move to suspend House of Representatives standing orders on 84 separate occasions in order to take up parliamentary time attacking her and her party rather than debating its legislative program. This tactic turned 'what had been a relatively rare occurrence into an almost daily spectacle' (Sydney Morning Herald, 6 Sep 2017, Adam Gartrell). According to Labor's Leader of the House at the time, Anthony Albanese, the Coalition proposed more suspensions in the 43rd Parliament than were proposed in the previous 42 parliaments put together (Gartrell). Mr Abbott eventually defeated Julia Gillard at the 2013 election, becoming Prime Minister on 18 Sep 2013. He was deposed less than two years later, on 14 September 2015, losing a leadership spill to Malcolm Turnbull.
¹⁰² On March 13, 2015 Mr Abbott, by then Prime Minister, was touring a Tasmanian farm when he grabbed and ate a raw onion, skin and all. The incident was filmed and widely disseminated, perplexing constituents and commentators and drawing international bewilderment: **https://www.news.com.au/lifestyle/real-life/wtf/i-shouldnt-have-eaten-an-onion-abbotts-biggest-regrets-as-prime-minister/news-story/46c1415282d57e038ba25be189cf7afb**, Liz Burke for news.com.
¹⁰³ Julia Gillard's partner Tim Mathieson is a business owner and hairdresser.
¹⁰⁴ The orator Cicero was, at the time of his assassination in 44BC, the most powerful public speaker and debater in the Roman world, and had directed many of his most devastating polemics at Marc Antony. Roman historian Dio states that after death, Cicero's head and hands were removed and set to be displayed on the speaker's platform in the Forum, but before being taken there the head was first delivered to Marc Antony at home, whereupon *'Antony uttered many bitter reproaches against it ...[a]nd [his wife] Fulvia took the head into her hands before it was removed, and after abusing it spitefully and spitting upon it,*

set it on her knees, opened the mouth, and pulled out the tongue, which she pierced with the pins that she used for her hair, at the same time uttering many brutal jests.' – Cassius Dio, *Roman Histories* 47.8, as quoted in 'Unsexing Fulvia' by Suzanne Dixon: **http://dangerouswomenproject.org/2016/07/19/unsexing-fulvia/**. See also Beard, Mary, *Women and Power* (Profile Books, London, 2017) pp. 43, 102; and **https://lydiaslibrary.wordpress.com/2014/10/02/ciceros-tongue/**.

BA   BY JOY

[105] This poem is an erasure of a media statement made by then-deputy Prime Minister Barnaby Joyce on 13 Feb 2018. Film of the second half of the speech can be viewed here: **https://www.theguardian.com/australia-news/video/2018/feb/13/barnaby-joyce-makes-public-apology-to-family-partner-and-voters-video**. Joyce's statement was actually about the scandal surrounding the end of his marriage and his relationship with a Liberal Party staffer, who was pregnant with his child at the time. It has been erased so that it comments on another 'deeply personal' issue around marriage: the divisive, painful and legally unnecessary same-sex marriage plebiscite of 2017. Joyce was one of the loudest voices in Australian politics calling for the plebiscite, even when other Coalition members and his own Prime Minister were equivocal. See for example: 'Nationals leader Barnaby Joyce won't compromise, he wants plebiscite', by Matthew Killoran, *The Courier-Mail*, September 26, 2016 **https://www.couriermail.com.au/news/queensland/nationals-leader-barnaby-joyce-wont-compromise-he-wants-plebiscite/news-story/afab1e4ed966765e31204df5dbc36d37**.

R E   ME   MBER 2017

[106] This is an erasure of Don Burke's public statement of 26 November 2017. Mr Burke made his statement in response to a joint ABC-Fairfax News story alleging he had sexually harassed staff on the Nine Network television program Burke's Backyard over a number of years. For more information see this news story: **http://www.abc.net.au/news/2017-11-27/don-burke-accused-of-sexual-harassment-indecent-assault/9188070**.

TOTAL FABRICATION

[107] This poem is a cut-up composed solely of words and phrases from Don Burke's public statement of 26 November 2017. See previous note.

TWO-HOLE BLUES

[108] 'Two-hole' is a violently misogynist slang term for 'woman'. All material in the first 6 stanzas of this poem is sourced from the Random Rape Threat Generator at **http://rapeglish.com/**, a resource compiled by academics Dr Emma A Jane (UNSW) and Dr Nicole Vincent (Macquarie University, UNSW) from hundreds of real-life misogynist messages involving death or rape threats, and/or particularly sexually explicit rhetoric, collected over a period of 18 years.

The peculiar misogynist idiom used to make these threats, christened 'Rapeglish', can be broken down into the following interchangeable components:
   Salutation - adjective + noun - punctuation (optional) - transitional phrase - outcome part 1 - outcome part 2

In order to avoid any prosecution for making actual violent death threats, the 'outcomes' are almost always expressed as either:
- orders for the recipient to do something of her own accord which will result in violence to her; or
- 'hopes' that something violent will happen to the recipient.

Actual examples:
- 'Fuck you, you unrapeable cunt, I hope you die of pussy cancer while your children watch, coz you're a stupid feminist asshole'
- 'Hey, you bitter hole, get back in the kitchen and drink bleach while anal sex wipes the smirk off your face, coz you need an attitude adjustment'

In the poem, all the misogynist statements have been changed from the second to the first person to underscore this feature of Rapeglish. See further Jane, Dr Emma A, *Misogyny Online: a Short (and Brutish) History* (Sage, 2017).

SUPREME GENTLEMAN

[109] This poem was created from the transcript of Elliot Rodger's video 'Retribution'. Rodger uploaded the video to YouTube on May 23 2014, the day before he murdered six people and seriously injured 13 others in Isla Vista, California. He ended by turning the gun on himself. His actions made him somewhat of a hero to lonely men in the self-styled 'incel' ('involuntarily celibate') community (Ford, Clementine, *Boys Will Be Boys* (Allen & Unwin, 2018), pp. 193-198). Transcript sourced from the LA Times May 24 2014: **http://www.latimes.com/local/lanow/la-me-ln-transcript-ucsb-shootings-video-20140524-story.html**. The text was then manipulated using the heroku glass leaves text manipulation app at **http://glassleaves.herokuapp.com/** (in particular, the 'get nouns and adjectives' manipulation).

ONLY FAIR

[110] This poem was also created from the transcript of Elliot Rodger's video 'Retribution' (see previous note). The text was then manipulated using the heroku glass leaves text manipulation app at **http://glassleaves.herokuapp.com/** (in particular, the 'create Markov chain' manipulation, which works a little like predictive text on a mobile phone).

ORION AS A WOMAN UNHELPED BY WHITE RIBBON

[111] The form of this poem is based on the constellation of Orion as seen from the southern hemisphere during our summer (with the red giant Betelgeuse in the lower right). Each stanza of the poem is positioned consistently with a star in the constellation, and the named stars are indicated with labels. The events in the poem are based on a real news story from the UK but have been transposed to this hemisphere and fictionalised. This poem was exhibited as an artwork (with the stanzas placed in their constellation positions on the body of a black dress) in the Belconnen Arts Centre exhibition *Postcards from the Sky*, Feb 8 - Mar 17, 2019 (see p. 38).

EURYDICE'S LAST SKY

[112] The form of this poem is based on the constellation of Virgo as seen from the southern hemisphere during our winter. As with the preceding Orion poem, each stanza of the poem is positioned consistently with a star in the constellation. Virgo was chosen because it was prominent in the sky above Melbourne at the time of the 2018 murder of comedian and writer Eurydice Dixon. The events in the poem are based on news reports of the murder and subsequent statements by authorities. This poem was exhibited as an artwork (with the stanzas placed in their constellation positions on the body of a black dress) in the Belconnen Arts Centre exhibition *Postcards from the Sky*, Feb 8 - Mar 17, 2019 (see p. 39).

BIOGRAPHIES

MELINDA SMITH is an Australian poet, editor, teacher, arts advocate and event curator based in Canberra, Australia. This is her seventh poetry publication. Her work appears nationally and internationally in literary journals and has been widely anthologised and translated into multiple languages. She has been awarded a number of prizes and grants for her work, including a Bundanon Trust residency, multiple ArtsACT grants, a Neilma Sidney Literary Travel Grant and the Australian Prime Minister's Literary Award. She frequently collaborates with artists in other disciplines including dancers, musicians and visual artists, and has appeared at literary and arts events all over Australia and in New Zealand, Italy and Japan. She is also a former poetry editor of *The Canberra Times*.

DR CAREN FLORANCE is a typographic artist and writer who currently lives and works in Canberra, Australia. She has produced a number of fine press letterpress books and broadsides featuring poets such as Rosemary Dobson, Nan McDonald, Les Murray and NZ poet Sue Wootton. Her recent practice-led doctorate explored the overlaps of visual poetry, text art and artist books. She has collaborated with Melinda Smith for a number of years, including on a public Variable Message Board project called 'Signs of Life' for the 2018 Contour 556 public art festival in Canberra. Caren's work is in national and international collections, mostly libraries. You can find out more at **www.carenflorance.com**

www.ingramcontent.com/pod-product-compliance
Lightning Source LLC
Chambersburg PA
CBHW060530010526
44110CB00052B/2551